A Photo Journey with

the American Kestrel

Lois Lake

Photographs by Lois Lake.

ISBN 978-1-943650-18-7

Library of Congress Control Number 2016933938

Published by BookCrafters, Parker Colorado.

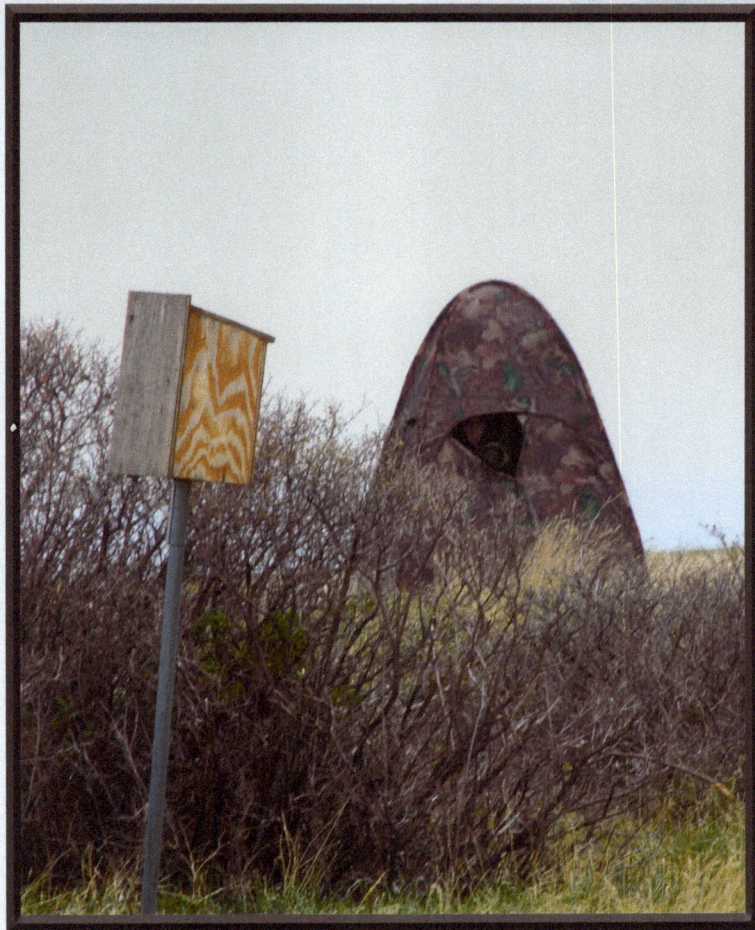

This is where it all begins.

I want to thank my husband, Steve Lake, for building a kestrel nesting box and putting it in our back yard. The nesting box brings the kestrel in and each year they stay for approximately one hundred twenty days while they raise their young. I put up a blind so I can sit quietly and observe them and take pictures without interrupting their behavior or causing them stress.

Please join me as we go on a photo journey
with the American kestrel.

The American kestrel (Falco sparverius) is the smallest falcon in North America and is also commonly known as the sparrow hawk. They are only nine-twelve inches long. The female has rust colored feathers on her back while the male has rust colors with slate-blue on his wings. You will often see them perched on highline wires, fences, or fence and telephone posts hunting for food below. Frequently, they hover with rapid wing beats while searching for lizards, grasshoppers, dragonflies, mice, voles, and snakes. They commonly return to their territory established the previous year for nesting. Kestrels do not build a nest for themselves, but rather use an old dead tree hollowed out by another bird or use a nesting box with cedar chips in it. Unlike most other falcons, both parents take turns incubating the eggs. There are generally three to five eggs per clutch and they hatch twenty-nine to thirty-one days after being laid. The young fledge in about thirty days, but they remain close to the nest for another twenty to twenty-five days, still depending upon the adults to provide a majority of their food. As their hunting skills develop they venture farther from the nest and catch their own food.

Hovering to hunt
for food.

One year, in early March, we saw a pair of kestrels mating on the north fence of our property. We quickly went on the internet and found a pattern for a nesting box. Steve built it and put it up on a metal post in the pasture.

Within a few days we noticed the male on the box. It appeared that he was checking out the territory for safety and food before bringing his mate to look at it. I began keeping a journal of activity.

As I was working in the yard, several times I heard a "cry, cry, cry." Then I heard a "coo, coo, coo." I started paying more attention to their communications. The male kestrel was bringing food to the female and then he went into the box. When he came out, she twitched her tail several times and they mated. I later read that this ritual is called courtship feeding.

One morning I set up the blind and got my camera ready to take pictures of the kestrel when it returned from hunting. I caught a movement in the scrub oak bush and was surprised when a male flicker landed on the kestrel box. He looked all around and over the edges of the box. Then he went to the entrance hole and looked around. Soon he went inside. I wanted to leave the blind and chase him away, but I didn't know where the kestrel was and didn't want to scare it away, so I waited. Then a female flicker landed on top of the kestrel box. She was not there for more than a minute before the female kestrel flew in and chased her away. The female kestrel sat on top of the box guarding it. I wished I could talk to her and tell her that the male flicker went inside the house. I kept wanting to say, "Mama, check inside your house!"
After watching the female kestrel on top of the box for about ten minutes, I thought maybe the flicker had flown out and I had missed it. At least I was hoping. Then the female kestrel heard something and hopped down and looked over the edge of the box into the entrance hole. Immediately, the male flicker flew out of the box. I was just sick. He certainly was in the box long enough to do a lot of damage to the eggs.

I wanted so badly to check to see if the flicker had damaged the eggs, but I did not want to cause the kestrel to abandon the nest. Each day I watched and the kestrel continued coming to the nesting box so apparently she had not yet laid eggs. I took the blind down and continued to observe their behavior from our deck.

The flicker was also looking for a place to lay her eggs and raise their chicks.

A couple of weeks later I set up the blind again. The male flew to an old, dead tree branch and started calling that he had food. Immediately, the female came out of the nesting box, accepted the food and flew off to a fence post where she ate it. She then returned to the nesting box. I sat quietly waiting and watching. In about an hour, the male returned. He gave the "cry, cry, cry" announcing that he was there with more food. Again, the female immediately came out of the box and accepted the food and flew off to the top of a tree and ate it.

She then returned to the nesting box. It was obvious that the female was incubating the eggs so she could not leave the nest to hunt. The kestrel does not begin the incubation process until the last egg is laid.

I continued watching this feeding pattern and I remembered reading that you should avoid checking the nesting box during the first two weeks of the thirty-day incubation period. I watched their behavior from our kitchen window to try and determine if the eggs had hatched yet. After thirty days, I waited until I saw the female leave the box to accept food. I checked the nesting box and found three chicks. It appeared that they were about four to five days old. They were just getting peach fuzz that would eventually turn to feathers, but there was not enough to keep them warm. Thus, the female would only leave the nest long enough to accept food the male brought her and the chicks. The chicks were not old enough yet to chirp or make any noise.

This morning I waited for the male kestrel to bring food to the female. He came in, landed on the branch and called to the female that he had food. She immediately came out to get it, but a magpie also heard the food announcement. The magpie flew up to the branch and tried to take the mouse away from the female. She flew away and circled around the nest with the mouse in her mouth and then she landed in the top of a pine tree. The female tried to take the mouse into the nest but it was too large to fit the entrance hole. She struggled to grab hold of the entrance hole with her talons with the mouse in her mouth. The magpie flew in to try and take the mouse away from her or make her drop it. In desperation, the female flew away again and the magpie followed. This time, the male kestrel intervened and chased the magpie away. After resting in the top of the pine tree for a few minutes and getting a different grip on the mouse, the female was able to get it in the nest to feed the chicks.

The male kestrel leaving a dead branch to deliver the mouse to the female.

The female accepted the mouse and tried to take it into the nesting box, but quickly turned away because a magpie was right there trying to steal it.

I had been watching the kestrel feed the chicks for about two weeks when, one morning, I noticed their behavior was a little different. I saw the male kestrel land on a weed with a small snake in his beak. He did the "cry, cry, cry" to announce to the female that he had food. She immediately came out of the nesting box and accepted the food. In the past, she would take it in the box and stay for a while. I assumed she was tearing small bites off the prey for the chicks to eat or perhaps she was regurgitating food for the chicks. This morning she took the snake into the box and immediately came back out. I saw her fly away to hunt for food.

Apparently, the chicks are getting old enough to tear off their own food.

Both adults now hunt for food and bring it to the nest. As they approach the nest I hear the "cry, cry, cry" announcing they have food.

I can now hear the chicks squawk in response.

There is always an abundant supply of grasshoppers.

This year we also had plenty of dragonflies.

Each day the chicks squawked louder and louder when they knew food was coming. They were getting big and strong enough to grasp the perch near the entry hole on the inside of the nesting box. The more aggressive chicks would stick their heads outside the entryway, squawking loudly. It was like they were saying, "Feed me first, feed me first."

Spring is a time of
new life for all of
God's creatures and
the bull snakes were
no exception. The
kestrel must have
found the bull snake's
den.

The female kestrel caught a mouse. She gets a good, solid grip on the mouse with one talon while leaving the other talon free to grab on to the entrance of the nesting box. The mouse is large and heavy. Her legs are almost not long enough to reach around the mouse to latch on to the nesting box.

It is hard to lift the mouse into the box when the chicks are competing to see who gets the food first. The kestrel made several attempts, nearly dropping the mouse multiple times before she successfully got the mouse inside.

Since the kestrel is a falcon, they are birds of prey and consequently, other small birds often become a part of the kestrel's food source.

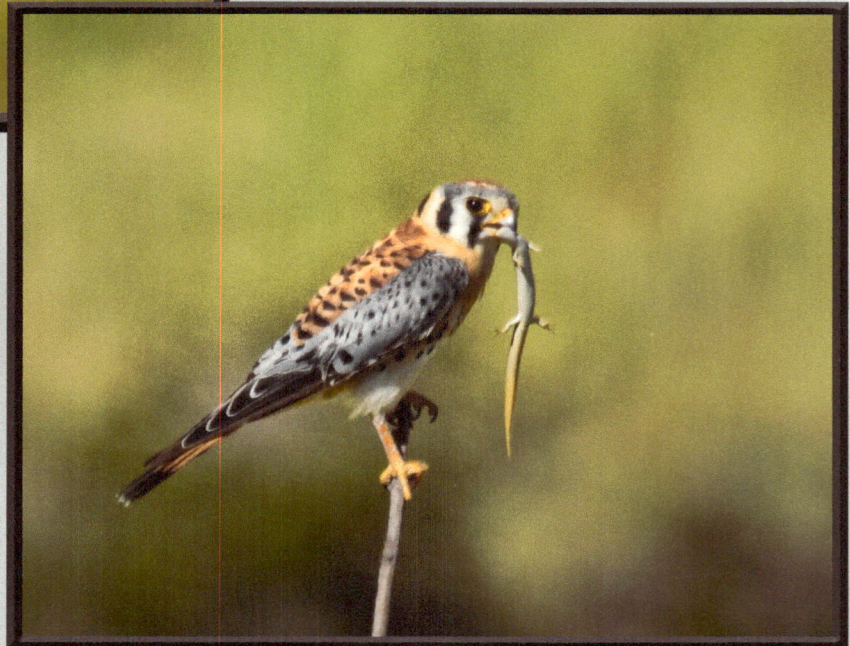

I have never seen a lizard on our property, but this year the kestrel found many of them. Lizards do not pee. Instead they produce uric acid which is secreted as a paste of microscopic white crystals. This makes it easier for kestrels to find them.

Crickets, centipedes and other small insects are a mainstay of the kestrel's diet.

The chicks come farther and farther out of the box to grab the food from the adult.

Two toes out the door. Every day they pushed the limit by getting just a little bit more of their body outside the box.

The chicks are becoming more vocal between each feeding. Their squawking for more food attracted the attention of the red-tailed hawk also looking for food for its baby.

This morning I heard a fast "cry, cry, cry, cry, cry, cry, cry."
I figured out that the fast cry and so many repetitions means
warning or danger. I started looking around. High overhead I
saw the red-tailed hawk soaring over the nesting box.
Apparently, he knows it is about time for the babies to
fledge. Both the male and female kestrel chased the red-tail
to protect their chicks. The chicks hid inside the box and not
a peep was heard.

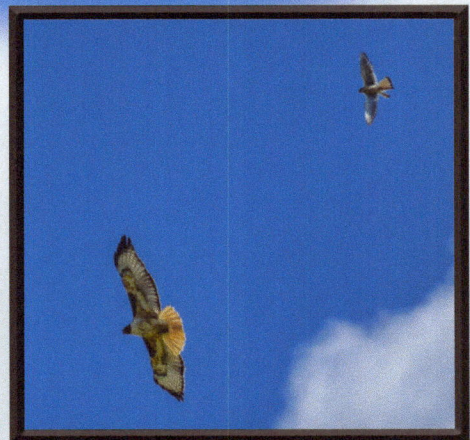

As I watched, I could almost read the chicks body-language. One seemed to say, "It is a long way down."

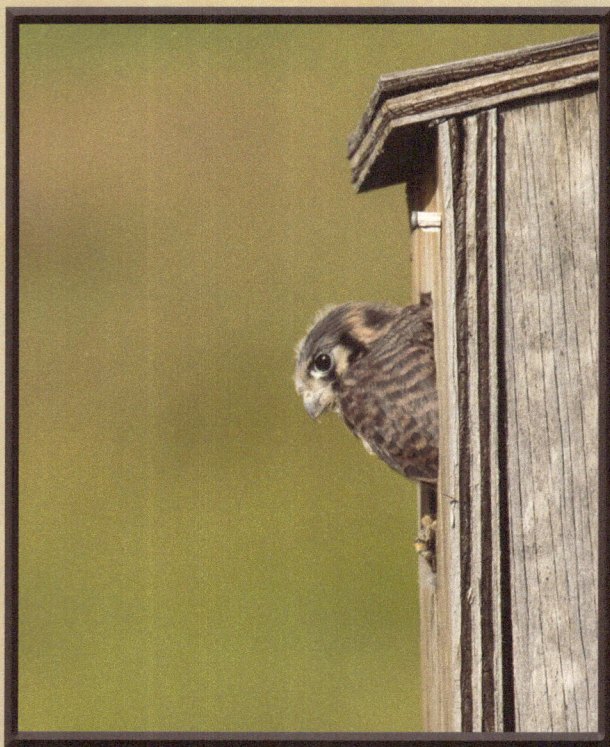

The other almost looks defiant about staying in the nesting box.

Each day the chicks jostled for position so they would be the first one to get the food. Occasionally, I could see two chicks perched together in the entry way.

The chicks had grown so much it was getting crowded inside the nesting box. I kept waiting for one chick to accidently push the other out of the nest.

The kestrel's behavior this morning was very different. The female announced that she had food, but she did not go to the box. She landed in a branch of a dead tree and did a "cry, cry, cry" to tell the babies she had food. They poked their head out of the box and started squawking, but she did not deliver the food. She flew around the box with a mouse in her mouth and landed on the tree branch again. I heard her, "cry, cry, cry" and then a "coo, coo." The male kestrel brought food to the babies and the female flew away with the mouse still in her mouth. The babies disappeared to eat the food that the male brought. In about thirty minutes the female was back with a snake announcing that she had food. She landed on the tree branch. I heard her, "cry, cry, cry" and then a "coo, coo." Then she flew around the nest with the snake while announcing that she had food.

She did this four times while I was there. It appeared that she was trying to coax the chicks out of the box.

I have food, but you have to come get it.

One morning, I heard the kestrel crying the warning/danger cry. I looked around to see what was happening. The female flew around our neighbor's house crying loudly and then she landed on the vent on top of their house. Kestrels rarely land on a house. They usually land in the top of a tree or on a fence post. Then I saw the male kestrel crying and flying around the neighbor's house. He landed on the peak of the roof. It was so unusual. I continued to watch and they were dive bombing the area around the choke cherry bushes. Then they landed on top of the house again. Their cry of warning/danger continued non-stop for over forty-five minutes.

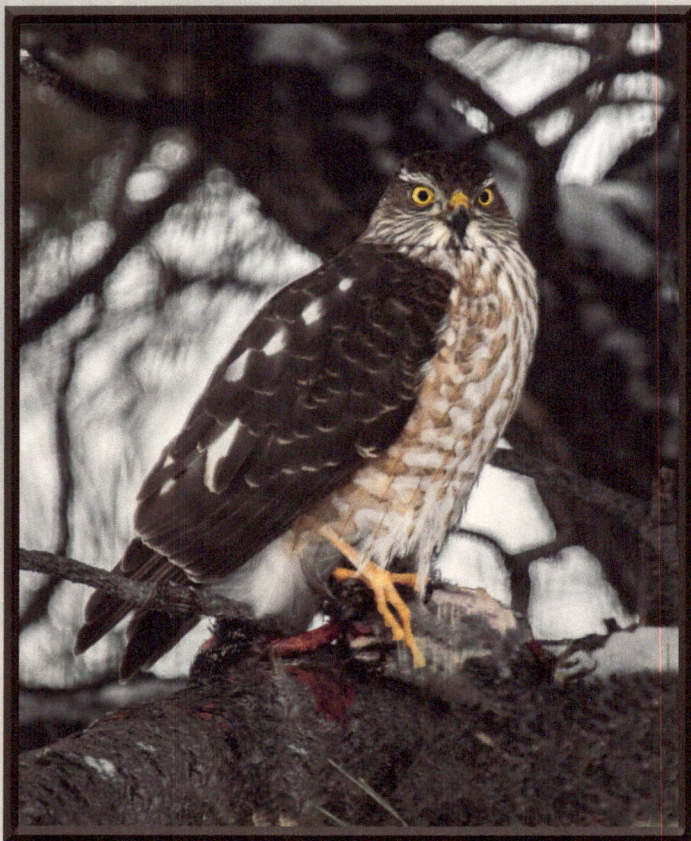

Then I saw a large, brown, bird fly from the choke cherry bushes to the tall pine tree in the gully. I believe it was the Cooper's hawk that I have seen before perched in our pine tree eating its prey. After it flew away, the kestrels settled down and started feeding the babies again.

At breakfast this morning I noticed the magpies gathering around the kestrel box. I wondered, "How do they even have a fighting chance?" I watched more closely and then I noticed one of the kestrel babies perched in the top of the scrub oak near the box. When the magpies got close the baby jumped to the center of the bush and dove down to the ground to get away from the magpies. I grabbed my camera and went out to watch and see what happened. As I set up my camera, I caught a movement out of the corner of my eye.

There was a second baby kestrel near the scrub oak on the left and I saw the third still in the nesting box. I decided to hang around to see if the babies were going to find their wings and how far they could fly.

I heard the adult kestrel crying the warning/danger cry again. I turned around to look for the danger and coming around the corner of our house, flying straight toward me and in the direction of the baby kestrel was a Cooper's hawk. The adult kestrel was in hot pursuit right on its tail. When it saw me it turned and headed toward the choke cherry bushes by the neighbor's house.

I turned my attention back to the baby that had not yet fledged. She poked her head out and stretched her neck. I could tell she was ready to leave the nest so I stood there and watched as she flew for the first time from the box to one of the short pine trees.

The landing was awkward and it took her a little time to get her balance.

The babies began squawking to let the adults know where they were and that they were still hungry.

I saw the female adult sitting on the neighbor's garden fence with food in her mouth. She gave the "cry, cry, cry" to announce that she had food. The chicks hopped from branch to branch trying to get a little closer to the food.

The chicks made short flights from one tree to another within an hour. When they landed they squawked for food. Each time the adult brought food, it would land farther and farther away from the chick to encourage it to fly.

One chick saw a grasshopper on the ground.

She recognized it as one of the foods the adults had brought and she hopped down to try and catch it. It is going to take some practice to refine that skill.

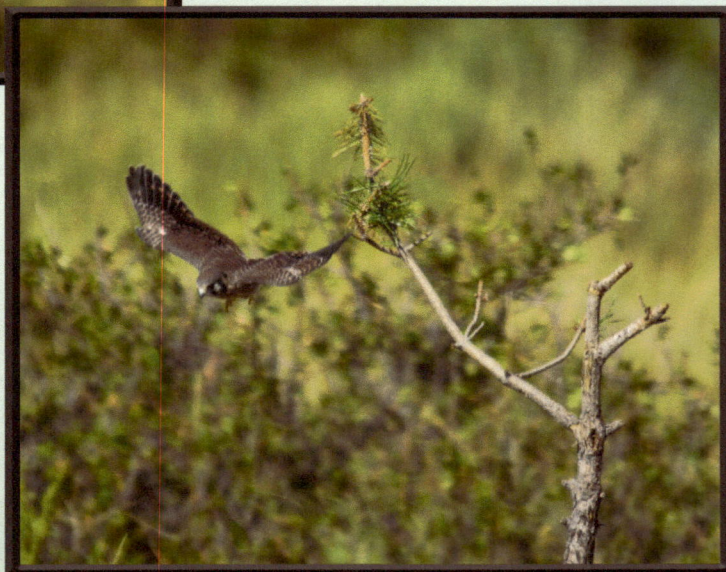

Later, the adult male kestrel came in and landed next to one of the babies on a branch of the small dead pine tree. It was like he was saying, "watch me and do what I do." He flew to the top of the large pine tree in the gully and the baby followed. In a very short time the chicks were taking longer and longer flights. Over the next couple of weeks, the chicks became less dependent on the adults for their food. I knew now that they had a fighting chance for survival and they were going to be safe.

I love to sit and watch nature.

It is fascinating to observe the way they communicate.
They have their own language, but some emotions are universal
across all beings. It was interesting that the kestrels had no
reservation in defending their chicks against the other hawks,
even though the red-tailed hawk was at least three times larger
than the kestrels. The kestrel uses its smaller size and agility
to its advantage. I often think we can learn so many lessons
by observing nature.

I consciously and deliberately used the dyslexie font type
to make it easier for people with dyslexia to read this book.

About the Author

Lois Lake grew up on a wheat farm on the great plains of Southeast Colorado. She discovered early that life is not always blue skies and sunshine, but it is full of opportunities. The key is to recognize those opportunities when they occur and take advantage of them. The skills of survival acquired on a farm and her resulting philosophy of life carries over into her photography. Lois likes to capture the stormy moods of nature and scenes of what happens in the outdoors. She is fascinated with non-verbal communication and body language, particularly among wildlife and enjoys the challenge of trying to capture that non-verbal communication in a photographs.

www.ingramcontent.com/pod-product-compliance
Lightning Source LLC
Chambersburg PA
CBHW041240020426
42333CB00002B/33